What These Hands Remember

What These Hands Remember

Poems by

Margaret Koger

Cover design by Shay Culligan
Cover photograph and author portrait by Betty Rodgers

ISBN: 978-1-63980-189-3

Kelsay Books
502 South 1040 East, A-119
American Fork, Utah 84003
Kelsaybooks.com

What These Hands Remember is for readers everywhere who find comfort in reclaiming the delights and trials of innocence during these challenging times.

Acknowledgments

Thank you to the journals in which these poems originally appeared.

Auroras & Blossoms Creative Literary Journal: "Nothing So Beautiful"

BLYNKT: "Thanksgiving Feast," "Lucky Mama," "The Color of Love"

Cabin Fever: "Written in Backstitch"

Elpis Pages: A Collective: "Summer Apples," "Burnt by the Wind," previously "The Fruit of Her Womb"

Inprint: "Mama Says"

Hunnybee: "The Hunt"

Love Gone Askew, Rhetoricaskew: "Dragon Love," "Girl with a Hollyhock Doll"

Montucky Review: "Who Called Himself Black Sheep"

Mused: BellaOnline Literary Review: "Polishing Silver," "A Cup of Ceylon Tea," "A Christmas Stocking Story," "New Life in the Elms"

One Title: "Try This Beauty Recipe at Home"

Many thanks to Grove Koger and to my family, friends, and colleagues in the Whittenberger Teachers Writing Group, Poetry in the City of Trees, and the Live Poets Society.

Contents

Written in Backstitch

See where the sweet home sampler hangs?
A fat hen on white with a robin-blue egg
perched on a perfect running stitch heart
its point scrolled in branches end-stopped
by tiny red valentines where loving fingers
stumbled to border each heart-wall and stem.
The needle plunging and pricking tender skin
love snipped in times when her passion bled.
The frame is an altar with a quarter inch rabbet
the glass once whole has cracked in a corner.
This is the whole story, love cased in thimble
the haystacks of language in linen and thread.
A tale written in backstitch, chain and straight,
the cross and a thousand and one French knots.

Girl with a Hollyhock Doll

She inspects a tall stalk
plucks off a perfect blossom
a petal skirt for a formal gown.
She holds the flower steady
pierces the stem, sepal, carpel
a sturdy toothpick's woody
length standing tall to hold
a bud for dolly's head.

Smiling a shy holly smile
she preens and bows
to catch a caterpillar's eye
a charming prince to beguile
long past midnight's chime
to dance 'til lusty cocks crow
her someday sunrise dawning
her pistil pierced for love.

Mama Says

"You go out there and clean that yard."
But gusting wind in poplar trees high overhead
threatens to break them apart.
Branches to tumble and crash
all falling down on me—
I whisper in fear, "Yea, though I walk
through the valley of the shadow . . ."

My grandmother knelt here, parted roots
planted this curse. A hot woman
conjuring shade from Idaho sun-flames,
never imagining how forty years would age
her supple saplings, the knuckles of their branches
swollen and cracking just as her hands crippled.

Mama says, "Always cool breeze on this hill . . ."
but October's Indian summer blows heat
storms dead leaves. Then Mama says, "Clean!"
I rake and pray, but I am no Dorothy
no Toto in my basket, no magic yellow bricks
leading to a good witch.
Only black asphalt winding up coyote hills
and down the Snake River.

Scenes from the Attic

In the garden:
Tangles of raspberry canes hiding bull snakes. They're scary but I'm sent to weed the beans. Then my sister, Patience, yells, "Go ahead, dig." I say, "No carnations in the garden, Mama said." Grandma planted them anyway; she's like that, and maybe I only dreamt about pulling them up.

Out in the backyard:
Daddy's California friend the peddler, Oren Schutz, pulled in the drive with a truckload of oranges. The men talk and when it's dinner, Dad invites him. Mama's eyes roll; she whispers, "Not enough food."

At the table:
Oren eats half a loaf of bread with lots of butter. "I churned that!" I say, offering up strawberry jam. The green beans and meatloaf make it to the finish! Oren tells stories of lemons, figs, and palm trees. Later Mama asks, "Now how will I make lunches?"

We get new neighbors:
And bang! Right away the old man dies . . . and here comes his son on leave from the army, a good-looker, who falls in love with Prudence, my other sister. The church women *tch tch* about Patience since only old maids let little sisters marry first.

At the church:
Prudence wears a white lace wedding gown but the timing's rushed and there's chatter. I overhear *teehee,* nine months for most babies; first babies come anytime. I'm not sure what . . . Anyway, I wear a new yellow dress for the ceremony and light the candles, even though I hate losing my sister to *him.*

At another neighbor's house:
Summertime and I watch my grown-up friend Helen knitting sweaters and booties: pink, blue, yellow. Then one day she calls, "Come in," from the bed, and there's no more knitting until Halloween when "Trick or Treat?" I hear knitting needles click again. Mama shakes her head. "So soon?"

Fall arrives:
The carnations in the garden smell like pepper! Mama says they should have been corn or beans, but she's been on her feet all day sorting apples. Then one Sunday, just before the first hard frost, a crystal vase of red carnations appears on the dinner table. Or maybe I dreamt the crystal.

Spring Semaphore

We called the flowers *flags*
in our rural disregard for fancy—
flags being their customary name
according to family tradition.

After the tulips bloomed and faded
no more Holland or metaphors
for clunky wooden shoes or a boy
saving the whole world by holding
back the sea with one finger!

Then, and only then, the glory
of flags, of spring semaphore
spears sprouting from damp soil
spiky stems bursting to unfold
the *fleur-de-lis,* see Grandma
spoke a little French.

Flags of sun-drenched yellows
bridal whites and conceptions
of royal purple petals arching
like velvet capes above the open
throats of blossoms waiting
impatiently for bees to bring
their burdens of pollen.

We knew little of city talk
or a rainbow goddess like Iris
her rainy-day displays before
June's gardens of licensed tea
roses blooming on canes with
bare thorns so wicked, mothers
warned children, "Don't touch!"

Flags on our kitchen table
signaled spring with their sweet
perfume happily recalling those
bloody days of stalwart citizens
bringers of Democracy to all
bursting into revolution, crying
Liberté, égalité, fraternité!
Citizens cutting aristocrats down.

How we celebrated patriots
who came to love the imperial *iris*
the signature of spring we loved.

Lucky Mama

Every second Sunday in August
arriving straight after church
a family reunion potluck picnic.
Women in bright silky dresses
flip open their wicker baskets
spread the rough tables with cloth
fill the long rectangles with bowls
salads, beans, rainbows of Jell-O
platters loaded with chicken or ham
apple and berry and apricot pies
midnights of dark chocolate cream
for the nourishment of our bodies.
Too full! the men moan after eating.
Only the women stay on their feet
a whole year of news to be had
Geneva, the eldest, Aunts Mandy
and Della, nieces Vera and Esther,
Rhett and Sally—married brothers.
A circle of women wide enough
to round it all into a yeasty dough
punching the air out and kneading
rye bread stories in needlepoint
tatted roses and crocheted lilies.
How to raise eggplant and cabbage.
Oh! You didn't hear? Their barn
burned to the ground and say,
how is Dave's leg these days?
In the end his heart just gave out.
Sorry. We didn't know—
eyes lifted on high, hands to cheeks,
only Mama gazing down, inspecting
smatters of clover, hearty as weeds.

She'll step aside for a moment
and pluck out a four-leafed gem
so that when I tug her elbow
teary-eyed, "Look here," she'll say
handing her luck to me.

Helping Father with a Stray

Our day to irrigate the pasture,
my dog Buck locked in the barn.
I'm surprised Father carries a gun
lets the yellow hound follow.
I swing the shovel on my shoulder
its wooden handle towering.

He watches as I pry open the rows
shoving clods of parched soil aside
so water will moisten the dry grass,
but I don't know why we keep on
beyond the pasture, climbing past
the sod barn, its sagebrush ruins.

"Stay behind me," Father warns.
He raises the gun and fires.
Smoke stings my nostrils, ears
ringing, tuned to the stray's cry.
A pet from town that grew too big
or too strong—too mean or dirty
or just too much trouble after all.

The stray was only one of many
pets shoved from speeding cars
left to hunt, live off the land
catch themselves some mice,
but the yellow was no predator
too slow, hungry, bleary-eyed.
He'd come, sidling into the yard
fighting Buck for table scraps
dog food not in our budget.

Father wipes tears from his eyes
and the rifle cracks again, twice.
When the whimpering stops
I step forward with my shovel
looking for a dry spot to dig in
away from the bloody testimony
of the mangy yellow's final run.

Lifting This Spoon

Scissors in Mama's hands trimming box-top coupons
Cheerios, Blueberry Muffins, we count the points,
5, 10, enough for a free spoon, but we need a fork.
Mama's hands writing a check for postage and handling
a piece-by-piece collection of Betty Crocker silver-plate.

And when the parcels come, we stand side by side
discard the cardboard, slide the spoons, forks, knives
into flannel pockets sewn from striped pajama scraps
banishing tarnish for up to twelve place settings
ready to grace an elegant table in Grandma's honor
her birthday perhaps. Or a Thanksgiving feast,
a new baby's arrival, the new year and oh, Easter!

Mama has picked "My Rose," but as I dream of mine,
my wedding rehearsal dinner? I choose "Affection."

Even on Sunday

Bullfrogs croak near lily leaves
spotted bodies dark and greeny
lazy white-legs loosely trailing
as wary eyes bumple in shallows
drift like shiny strings of beads.

A multitude of tiny frogs
throng on grassy banks and sing
sabbath *ribbet* rings of praise
but uh-oh take a step too close
and cries erupt in noisy *crrrroaks*
then *plop! plop!* into the pond!

A heron stands by a willow
his piercing stare into the pond
reflects his fervent prayer that
soon a chorus of tasty frogs
will stray within reach.

Then with a flash of his bill
and a gulp of his gullet, *baroo—*

Dragonflies on *whirry* wings
float above this still-life fray
a reminder to all who cannot fly
how some supremely do.

Frogs, herons and dragon flies
making a living. Even on Sunday.

Polishing Silver

Then
my hands knew what to expect
tugging the stuck lid open
lavender silver-polish
finely granular, faintly greasy.
Dip the worn white sponge
smear up a load and rub as you
hold dampened tableware tight:
spoons, forks, knives.

Now
my hands will ache from gripping,
joints a little stiff like Grandmother's.
I recall her spoon bowl center table
its blue and white porcelain curves
arches of willowy British branches
draped over a peaceful riverbank.
A bowl of silver-plate spoons
engraved McA in Scottish pride.

Then
Three years old I was, helping
Grandmother Neva set the table
with knives and forks at places
plates, bowls, glasses, napkins
all carefully balanced so Mother
could rest after work at the bakery
and big sisters home from school
would *have* to play with me
because I was a *good* girl.

Yes, when I polish silverplate
roses remind me of Grandmother's
yard full of flowers, lilacs and lilies
and the low limbs of loaded trees
bearing pie cherries and peaches.

My hands know those days
picking fruit and rubbing silver
tarnish blackening the sponge
tarnish washed down the drain
as my porcelain sinks remind me
of the chipped enamel dishpans
the single cold-water faucet
the teakettle whistling its boil
ready to pour into the wash pan.

Hands and cups buried wrist-deep
in foamy white suds welcoming
the after-dinner team of sisters
washing in strict order the glasses
china plates, silver, kettles, skillets.
The done dishwater flung in the alley
behind Grandpa's shabby toolshed
the flour-sack towels hung to dry
folded to show the days of the week
embroidered with washday Monday
ironing Tuesday, baking on Friday
our nimble fingers ready to rest.

A Christmas Stocking Story

I'd roll up one of my baby booties
and stuff it deep into a brand new
cotton sock and hang them both
to wait for Santa's midnight call
long past our evening supper-bowl
of creamy chowder topped with butter
churned from a Jersey beauty's bounty
for cows *give* milk to the nourishment
of our bodies and—"Thy will be done."
A child well-fed on a sacred night ate
biscuits heaped with peach preserves
sweets to shimmy up sugar plum
dreams of nights before Christmas
when all were to bed and Santa came
to fill our stockings, since Baby Jesus
he loved all the children of the world.

And then

morning and I'd dump my stocking.
There! The tiny bootie filled with gold
a fortune of foil-wrapped chocolate
coins as rich as frankincense, myrrh
and Mother, sweeping me into her arms,
holds bootie and stocking side by side
and says, "My how you've grown!"

A Cup of Ceylon Tea

I hold the teakettle high enough
above the burner so its whistle
whispers, hums, and throbs.
I hear again my father warning,
"Let the water boil—pour
straight into the cup."

He thinks only boiling water opens
tea leaves to the sunlight they recall
shining on a faraway hillside.

All day there the wind breathes in
comforting aromas, *Camellia sinensis*.
Warm scents as sweet and virginal
as blossoms of camellias in corsages
my sisters and I wear for dancing.

Tea raised in rows of green shrubs
narrow bands striping long tropical
slopes where even now someone
picks tea leaves that will someday
rustle into an infuser, be steeped
as I am in a childhood enigma:
"Let the water boil first."

Try This Beauty Recipe at Home

Washing and setting Mother's hair
hot and cold water blended to warm
her head lowered gently over the sink
a cotton cloth covers her eyes—no tears
shampoo suds piling in vibrant white
and the scents of clean hair rising.

When the swirling rinses run clear
you wrap her wet head in a terrycloth
turban and press gently to dry, unwind
and drape the towel on her shoulders.

The mother's sturdy white hair shines.
Now use a wide-tooth comb to separate
thick hair curving around pink rollers.
Curls to surround her wide hazel eyes
deep as the wells of love in Galilee.

Who Called Himself Black Sheep

If we bought a headstone
for Uncle Gene, it would not
be a polished marble monument
revealing his life on earth
as son or brother or husband;
nor would it be a bronze
celebration of his fight
for old men's causes.

If we bought a marker
for Uncle Gene, it would be quilted
in beds of flowers and onions
a tribute from his nieces
to pieces of life he let go.

"Girls," he'd say
on his way out the door
to somewhere else,

"What d'ya think?"

Waiting

Imagine outlining a story
one everyone hopes will come true
sooner rather than later. A sense
of the sky falling and something . . .
One glance across a crowded room
lights a girl's eyes; she's waited there
stuck like a salmon in a reservoir
nosing the limits of banked walls
breathing pooled water in and out,
in and out, over and over.

Then the muddy wall rolls open
the dam breached, the pool trembles.
She who is A edges into the stream
where she sees a shadow of B
who is sure to become her other half.

She imagines white wedding napkins
two hearts joined by a silver arrow
their names, Alice and Benicio below.

Then the writer will order more paper
for the lovebirds' C and D, and . . .

Dragon Love

I flew
a red-bellied dragon
pieces of reed, paper, wire
glued, ready to mount the sky.
He seized an updraft as I ran
his call fading from my ears.
I took his tether string to heart
wind gusts thumping tempos
pulse of boom and silence
his green lyrics soaring
sweeping me into
the blind eyes of
oncoming storms
boasting of fiery
bolts racing
down
his rag
and
silk
s
t
r
i
n
g
t
a
i
l

one with no key.

Nothing So Beautiful

Nothing is so beautiful as an orchard in spring
when limbs, in layers, spread wide and sweep
forces of petals, all pink, like everlasting promises,
blue of a captured sky, glories of blue eggs nestled
in nests of robin redbreasts who sing cheers!
Cheer up, cheerily, cheer up . . .

Comes a cat climbing. Sharp, sharp the bird beaks
rigid to peck, wings to whir, darting and dashing
the cat plunging, a race of claw-skids, down, down
until *crash!* echoing up through buds of apple-clings
scrapes of shredded bark to be sealed with xylem
flowing up from roots soaked in wet, hallelujah, soil.

Summer Apples

The power of spring sunlight
warmed the lips of twigs,
formed buds   unfolded blossoms
itching for bees to spread gold lamé
on their stigmas   pollen carrying
sperm down tubes   to ovules
as in so many female buds.

Surrounded by sheltering leaves
ripened apples invite our teeth
to bite into their crisp flesh
a tart dance on the tongue.

Summer apples meant to replace
barrels of root cellar has-beens,
only not quite   because the new girls
arrived before the berries were done.

We pick a few   bake pies   leave
the rest to tumble into weeds where
they'll be gathered to feed the hogs.

Some year there'll be a free-for-all
boys flinging their ardent desires at
side-stepping girls   or so I imagine.

I see the hogs   the trees   and me
as if I too were a giggly dancer
dodging apples   hoping a suitor
will come to court me   or else
the fruits of my body may be lost
left to rot   to brown in the sun
bees drunk on abandoned sugars.

The Hunt

It was an old garden full of dead fairies
statues of elves and sprites
chortling with glee
brandishing the weapons they'd used
to kill their fey, gadfly cousins.
Elves and sprites lurking among the flower beds
toeing toward your feet on the gravel path
ready to trip you. And then what?
You were supposed to solve the murders,
one said, and then take your choice of weapons
and stash one in your bag. But it was like looking
for the witch-maker's husband, peering
under the benches, over the tops of hollyhocks
seeing no one there.

As I struggled through the shadows
they hissed and I kept losing my mind.
Did the *sssss* or the *SSSSS* mean hot?
Should I follow a scent or spider web?
The tiny path into a maze of carrots?

Look here! A gnome appears—
like a statue, whispering,
not moving his lips.

The Color of Love

Heading home from the hospital
I cut through Pioneer Cemetery
a summer green-grass lawn where
crosses and headstones remark
here lies Cyrus, Alta, James
memorials jeweled by dew—
or wait . . . *tchk, tchk, tchk, tchk*
the sprinkler's skyward flow.

The water bursts from pipes
swish-swishes onto trees, leaves
the stream an arc on the horizon
against the foothills, sun wreaking
startles of rainbows quickly
red, orange, yellow, green, blue,
indigo, violet, red again, orange
disappearing, such as we do.

I think of my new grandson
in his heated hospital crib
barely aware of a new world
its earth, air, fire and water.

I whisper:
"Little one, in your far future days
when you walk among graves
or when rainbows catch your eye,
remember my love still colors
even now, even then, your world."

Thanksgiving Feast

I'm in with my grandson
at the preschool eating turkey,
cranberries, rolls oozing butter
giggling over pumpkin pie
our whipped cream mustaches.

As we head to the playground
his little hands grasp my arm
and kisses flow from his lips
muscle memories reclaiming
how he slept on my chest
when he was tiny and I waited
to feel him waking, neck strained
to lift his bob-bobbling head,
blue eyes slowly capturing
the where-am-I-now world.

Today
in the sandbox, he shovels,
sand flies into a red pail but
he stops to look up, make sure
I am still there. I'm backlit
a dark form, an outline of Nana.

I fear he'll see a monster shadow
but he blinks and settles back
shovel flying, as I wait to see
a castle, fort, rocket ship.

But it's only a pile of sand.
And we walk back inside
hand in hand.

Literacy with Dragons

At the zoo, my
five-year-old grandson
gazes at the signs
in front of cages
uses my ballpoint
clickety-click pen
to record his tour
A B C letters adding up
to animal names.

"Nan, what are these?"

RED-TAILED HAWK

GOLB (Meant a D)ENEGLE

And this one?

indiAn SARUS CRANE

RUFOUSCROWNED RO
LLER.

He writes in a souvenir
notebook I gave him
a present from Barcelona.
His findings encased
in a turquoise and orange
print of the cracked-plate
ceramic dragons
on benches at Park Güell.

Beasts in the faraway city
like
         ZOOBOISE's own

37

KOMODo DRAGON

lazing in the sun.

New Life in the Elms

You know how these trees used to be all lithe limbs and sexy leaves before so many decades waltzed by. Now look, see a few that still recall their earlier sweep and razzle-dazzle. Never mind those big bottom trunks—remember their limber tippy-toe sapling selves with swelling xylem links to roots spearing deep into fertile ground.

There you go! Looking into the canopy and swearing by the swept-up sight of crowns one-hundred-plus feet aloft. You bet—it would take twenty, thirty however many of you balanced one up and then another stacked head to toe impossibly high and still the highest one would be shaded by leaves layered between you and what we used to call heaven.

You know too that in fall one two four weeks and all those red and yellow leaves will drift down showing our bare branches while we wait out the winter season, sketches of crazy black bark, lines in alphabets not to be read or even looked up to, because these girls, we will very soon dress up in spring green satins swaying in trifle breezes and whisper—I, I, inside I'm still that lithe little sapling I was many moons ago.

Burnt by the Wind

Then
Neva   an eldest daughter   sent
to cook men's food   feed horses
follow the plow   her beauty
burnt by wind   while the sisters
wrote poems and painted portraits.

Now
A tang of acrid sage in my car
desert air pricked with memories
my grandmother resurgent
—risen from my blood.

I speed down the freeway
asphalt layered on wagon ruts
angled over restless ghosts.
Homesteaders denied water
runoff from dams diverted
crops dried in the fields.

An angry haunt in calico
she points to the past   *see   there*
dry washes   withered orchards
downed fences   an infant's grave.

Neva   the eldest daughter
to cook men's food   feed horses
follow the plow   beauty burnt.

How I would love to hold her
hear the piano   once more
thirsty fingers tapping like nails
on the keys, belling my years of
husbands and vanished aspirations.

But I believe she's young again
a soul immune to birthdays.
I love her here   in the desert
where new crops drink well water.

I feel how she spread her thighs
—to deliver *this*   my entire earth.

About the Author

Margaret Koger grew up on a small ranch in Idaho after electricity spread across the land but before her family could afford a well. Water for drinking and washing had to be hauled from town and stored in a cistern, creating a lesson in water conservation not to be forgotten. Her dad traded used tires for her first pony. She received her M. A. from Boise State University and continues to live in Boise, where she taught in the public schools, specializing in creative writing and library services with a brief stint as an Artist in the Schools. She is a Lascaux Poetry Prize finalist, and more of her work may be found in the Boise City Department of Arts and History COVID Community Collection, *Amsterdam Quarterly, Chaffey College Review, Burning House, Tiny Seeds Literary Journal, Topical Poetry, Elpis Pages: A Collective,* and *The Limberlost Review.*

www.ingramcontent.com/pod-product-compliance
Lightning Source LLC
Chambersburg PA
CBHW031009090426
42737CB00008B/741